New Zealand

Long White Cloud

Stephen and Scharlie Platt

www.leveretpublishing.com

New Zealand: Long White Cloud

First published - August 2017
Published by
Leveret Publishing
56 Covent Garden, Cambridge, CB1 2HR, UK

Maori chief's death mask, Museum of New Zealand (Te Papa Tongarewa) Wellington

ISBN 978-0-9957680-5-5

New Zealand
Long White Cloud

Abel Tasman Trail, Mutton Cove to Totoranui

New Zealand 2012

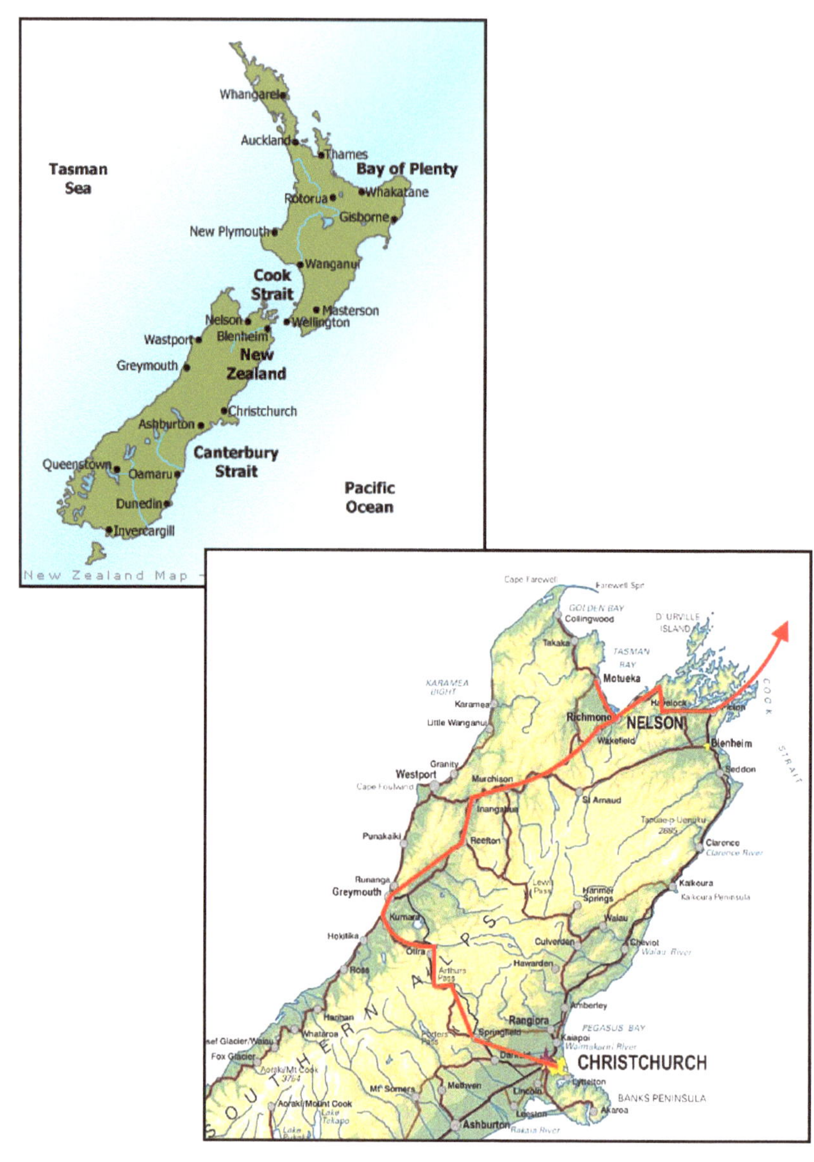

Christchurch

Tuesday 14 February

In Christchurch airport there were signs everywhere saying any plant material would be destroyed and there would be a fine of $400. Scharlie remembered the large eucalyptus seeds she had secreted in a sock in her checked in luggage and couldn't decide whether to declare them or throw them away. Finally she fished them out of her luggage and found a bin we could throw them in before the cases were screened. The delay meant we were almost the last through customs and in the kerfuffle Scharlie left her purse behind. Luckily an air hostess came through customs with it.

There was a thin fit-looking man in a flat hat holding a card with our name; it was Scharlie's cousin John. You must be the last off, he said. I haven't seen Scharlie for nearly sixty years, but I thought you were the only possible couple. We didn't explain why we were late. John drove us into Christchurch, having to think hard about how to navigate the temporary road layout after the

Molly and John Andreae, our hosts in Christchurch

earthquake the previous year, which had closed off large parts of the town centre. This was a major event, causing185 fatalities and extensive property damage and as part of my research on disaster recovery I was keen to learn how the authorities were managing the recovery. My plan was to contact and interview all the main decision makers and we also planned to tour the damaged areas and make a photographic record of the damage with a GPS camera for another research project back at the office in Cambridge. At home we were warmly welcomed by Molly with old-fashioned English manners. She said she remembered being fascinated by Scharlie's 12-year-old Jamaican accent but we couldn't hear a trace of Kiwi in hers.

Wednesday 15 February

The next two days passed in a flurry of work trying to contact people to interview to learn about recovery planning after the earthquake. There was no wireless access and John kindly lent Steve his computer. With help from John Peet, a friend, and Andy Buchanan, a friend of a colleague in Cambridge, Steve started to make contacts and began telephoning people in the local government and the university. Reading reports in the press we began to learn about the complex interactions between the city council and the various

Looking towards the damaged Christchurch Cathedral. the centre closed to public

other planning bodies and the worries and uncertainties of ordinary people.

It was unseasonably cold, with condensation on the windows, and the heating on. Apples and roses and fuchsias in the garden – it's late summer here. Much of the rest of the day Steve spent on two trips to Westfield shopping mall to get money from an ATM and a Sim for his phone. It was important to get the phone connected to the Internet to make contact with useful informants.

In the evening Malcolm, Steve's friend from school and climbing partner at university, came with his wife Doreen and drove us to Sumner, a resort suburb to the east. We walked up the road to the landslip where the headland had disappeared into the sea, and then back along the promenade. Malcolm was a mine of information about New Zealand. His daughter Kate lives in Christchurch and his brother, Norman, in Canberra. Kate's house was badly damaged in the quake. We went for a drink in a temporary bar constructed using a shipping container and a leanto marquee, with an artificial grass floor and tables made from beer barrels. The wine was good, so we bought a bottle as a present for John and Molly, and went on to a Thai restaurant for dinner. Malcolm began to explain a little about life here and to describe a society seemingly so English on the surface, yet so different geologically and culturally.

Malcolm and Scharlie walking along the promenade in Sumner

The Maori are quite different from the Aboriginals in Australia, he explained. They were warlike and highly organised and wrestled the Treaty of Waitangi from the British Crown in 1840. Now they are the business class and powerful in arguing about their ownership of coastal rights and farmland.

Thursday 16 February

The following morning Steve continued emailing and in the afternoon we surveyed in Murray Ainslie and Hillsborough suburbs that had been badly affected by the earthquake in the Port Hills to the east of John and Molly's house. We had a map with three study areas and a GPS camera to take photos of houses and buildings to help identify construction materials. Steve drove and Scharlie photographed through the window.

We got back and dressed to go to a concert in the new Court Theatre. The old theatre had been damaged and $4 million had been raised to build a new temporary theatre in Addington in an old warehouse. John said it was much better – better seats, better stage and better acoustics. The show was 'Side-by-Side by Sondheim' with a medley of Stephen Sondheim's hits. We made it in good time and milled around in the foyer. The audience mainly comprised older people and Molly met lots of friends while John, being more retiring,

Scharlie photographing building damage using office GPS camera

retreated outside. Steve joined him and enjoyed the evening sun.

We were very taken by the set design – large frame panels with some translucent material and hidden perimeter LED lights that change colour. The effect was of a derelict warehouse. The players were two pianists at grand pianos, a narrator in white suit and pointed white shoes and two women and a man. They were good and the voices of the women melded well. After the interval the scenery was swivelled to produce a New York skyline and one realised that the symmetrical framing of the panels created a 3-D effect. During the interval we wandered around looking at the architecture. The theatre was a box inside the warehouse constructed from a steel frame and sandwich panels with some kind of absorbent filling about 4 inches thick. There was a bar, ticket office and coffee shop made from shipping containers painted bright red. This re-use of brightly painted containers with smart fittings is the theme of the temporary reconstruction in Christchurch and later we got to know who were the designers – Fulton Ross Team Architects.

Steve managed to arrange to see Diane Turner second-in-command at CERA, the Canterbury Earthquake Recovery Authority, at 8.30 the next morning. He also sent out emails asking to see Roger Sutton the CEO of CERA and finally managed to arrange an interview over the phone.

The new Court Theatre, housed as an acoustic box inside a ruined factory

Friday 17 February

John kindly ran Steve into the HSBC building opposite the art gallery I was early so went to a coffee shop on the ground floor and ordered a machiato. I was nervous and excited by the prospect of getting started and had been waiting a while when I realised that they must have forgotten my order so I went to the counter and asked. The barrista said they usually charge for their coffees. I said I tried to pay but thought I'd been told to sit and be served. The coffee was undrinkable.

Diane was a tall striking woman with black hair and red lips. She introduced me to Julian Carver, who is in charge of IT. She was affable but very sharp and gave me an overview of CERA's role and the state of play and then said she'd leave me with Julian as she had to fly to Auckland for a meeting with the Minister to discuss the plan for the Central Business District. It had become clear from talking to people on the phone that this plan was one of the most controversial aspects of the reconstruction. This isn't a drawing, as one might imagine, but rather a set of rules that will govern rebuilding and spatial ordering of activities. An extensive consultation with the general public has led,

Performace of 'Side by Side by Sondheim'.

she said, to a plan for a low rise, greener inner-city. It is apparent, however, that since the whole of the centre is cordoned off, businesses have had to relocate, many to Riccarton and near the airport to the West. Property owners and the business community have submitted their own response to the central business district plan. Diane left me with Julian and he described how they were going about creating a database. He had been a consultant providing IT advice to the private sector and government. He said New Zealand was advanced in IT and that companies tried new products here, since if they worked in a market of 4 million they were likely work elsewhere.

We also talked about walking. Scharlie and I planned to go trekking once I'd finished my study. Julian said his family came from Keswick. He said he had been to the Lakes and thought the mountains were a joke. I didn't argue. I did some more surveying before finding the bus terminal and a bus to the University to have lunch with Andy Buchanan in the Engineering Faculty. The bus station is in Tuam Street behind Ballantyne's department store. I went to the ticket counter and asked if there were concessions for over 65. The girl exclaimed you're not that old are you? You don't look it. I said that's the nicest thing anyone said in ages. The drive took us past endless brash commercial outlets in cheapjack

Catching the bus in Tuam Street

buildings. The University is in a green campus and majors on science and engineering. Andy came and found me and took me around the labs where they are doing earthquake research and showed me a huge test rig. There was a section of a concrete post and beam structure that had interesting triangular release sections providing a gap at the end of each beam where it joined the column to allow the building to rock without causing damage. The surface of the concrete was covered in sensors and coloured wires. Andy introduced me to a young Asian lad who was doing an experiment with a novel timber structure. It was lunchtime and in the staffroom over coffee I bought an edition of the New Zealand Earthquake Society Journal for Robin for $30, thinking more weight to carry. Andy helpfully set up more meetings for me, one with an engineer at Tonkin and Taylor, the engineering firm responsible for much of the investigative boreholes and the land and building survey work. He rang an ex-PhD. student, Bruce Dean who is in charge of building the GIS database. He also rang Rod Cameron at SKIRT, responsible for infrastructure repair and an architect Jasper Van Lingen who is currently president of the local architects association. Andy had to meet someone so there wasn't really time to talk about walking. He is a keen tramper and wanted to give us some tips about where to go and suggested that we come to his house for tea on Sunday so

Christchurch Cathedral, initial decision to demolish being reconsidered by Anglican Church

we could talk then. I got back on the orbital bus that stopped at the bottom of the hill, and walked up the steep side road to home.

That afternoon John and Molly lent us their car to go surveying in the Mount Pleasant area and we did a couple of hours before we had to get back to be ready for dinner with two friends of Molly and John, Catherine and John Peet, and Dorrie and Tim, Scharlie's sister and brother-in-law, who were also visiting from England. It was sunny and warm and we drove up high into the Port Hills until we came to a sign saying that the summit road was blocked. We were getting into the routine of surveying now. We got back in good time and Scharlie got ready while Steve checked his emails. Our guests arrived and we sat around rather formally in the living room while John served drinks and Molly worked in the kitchen. She came out to help him and then suddenly cried out when she realised that the sauce was burning. John ran to help and she closed the sliding doors to deal with the crisis in private. Catherine said we should carry on talking. Tim and Dorrie have been seeing much more of the island than we have and arrived for dinner fresh from having visited Milford Sound. They had lovely weather, the only drawback being that because there has been a drought for nine days the waterfalls are not as spectacular as normal. They are staying with friends and using Christchurch as a base and

Canterbury Provincial Council Chamber, Benjamin Mountfort, (1865) being demolished

are whale watching tomorrow. We asked John Peet about his thoughts on anti capitalism, since John had mentioned that this was a new passion of his. He said he was against growth rather than anticapitalist. I felt like suggesting that was all right with people like us but that growth might be necessary for young people to get on in life. But wisely I kept my mouth shut. Molly had rescued the sauce somehow and the meal was good. Catherine talked about how she ran workshops and how she always began by asking people what they most valued – family, friends, walking, beach and then she pointed out that these things didn't have a monetary value. They kindly offered to give us a key for their bach on Arthur's pass.

Saturday 18 February

The following day was Saturday and since we had managed to fix appointments for Monday and Tuesday we could relax and take time off. We got up early again. John had lent is the car and we drove to the Banks Peninsular. The road was straight at first, passing through farmland, the pastures not unlike England but the trees darker and more sombre. We came to a range of hills separating us from the coast and climbed through steep curves until we began to drop

Duvauchelle Bay Banks Peninsula

down towards Akaroa – a pleasant sleepy seaside town with picturesque wooden houses and a few shops and cafes, its setting, beside a bay stretching inland, almost like a fiord but wide and sheltered.

John had recommended Hinewai Nature Reserve and that we meet a friend of his who runs it. At the gate a man with a Geordie accent invited us in and we learnt that John's friend was away collecting seed from a tree newly discovered in South Island and previously thought to be extinct. The man said he had a patch of land over the brow of the hill on the edge of the reserve. The reserve is huge and stretches over two river valleys from the brow of the ridge and the road we'd driven up almost to the coast, but the final headland pastures were owned by the Armstrongs. We descended a mown grass path as far as the visitor centre and warden's house where he lives in the most Spartan fashion, only occupying part of the house.

The visitor centre was well appointed with a wood stove, half a dozen bunks, kitchen and compost loo. From the information about the history of the reserve we learnt that it had been a sheep farm, but had been abandoned. From the wall map we decided on a circular walk that encompassed the central part of the reserve and set off downhill. The rainforest, or what is called 'bush', is lush with tree ferns, cabbage tree and flax. A sign explained that

Scharlie on the way to Hinewai Nature Reserve

there was a problem with the gorse that had been imported from the UK as hedging but had become rampant and killed off the native vegetation. The previous owners had tried to control the gorse by burning but that had only encouraged it. The new plan was to use the gorse as a nurse crop to shelter native trees like black beech, which, when tall enough, would shade out and kill the gorse. It seemed to be working in some places, but there had been a fire a year ago, which had run through all the higher land on the ridges and although the vegetation was coming back, some years of growth had been lost. What has been achieved is most impressive and may be having an influence on the neighbours, some of whom have designated parts of their land as conservation areas that they are allowing to revert to bush.

The path went down and down and we wondered about the climb back. We crossed the stream and climbed the steep bank using a ladder. At the top Steve turned and found that Scharlie was nowhere to be seen. Finally she called. She had turned the wrong way up the stream but luckily had realised and stopped. We could hear bellbirds and got views across the wooded gorge and up to the outcrops of the Stony Bay Peak. Birds flew across the valley with a rising and falling flight, rather like wood pigeons. Finally after a tiring ascent we reached the grassy track which took us back.

Overlooking the Hinewai Nature Reserve

Driving down to Akaroa we parked in front of the supermarket and bought bread and cheese for lunch. The road names and architecture reflect the French influence of the original settlers – the houses have ornate balconies and wooden verandas. We went for coffee in a garden cafe and sat in the dappled shade of the eucalyptus and decided to try and reach Stony Bay. We drove up to the Maori longhouse, or Marae, and little church Catherine had mentioned, but there was a wedding in progress, with guests outside the church waiting for the bride, and it seemed private, so we didn't linger.

After a false start in the wrong direction we discovered the right road to Stony bay in the middle of the village. The road was steep and unmade and wound its way up the hills in steep curves. This is cattle country but, as Malcolm had explained, the pasturing regime is different here and sheep and cattle are concentrated in a single field at a time because the land generally needs irrigation and it's more efficient to graze the fields in strict rotation. Scharlie was worried by the precipitous drop on her side of the road and the prospect of damaging John's car, so we went slowly and the car's small engine laboured. Finally we reached the coll, parked and got the lunch out. We chatted to a young French couple we had offered a lift to lower down but who had walked all the way. A sign said 40 minutes to Stony Bay Peak –

Stony Bay from the col where we picknicked

an easy climb with a wonderful view – so we put on our walking shoes and walked up a narrow path through the charred gorse to the rocky top and a view of the Bay. We lingered awhile and then descended the same way back.

A jeep arrived at the parking place in a cloud of dust. The man driving said he'd come to paraglide but the wind was too strong. They usually took off from just above and flew through the gate at the height of the pass. He seemed very hacked off and roared off again the way he'd come, telling us that the road down to Stony Bay was worse. Feeling intrepid we continued on the track down to Stony Bay and were rewarded with a panoramic view of sea and rocky cliffs below grassy headlands. In fact it wasn't anywhere near as bad as we expected and not as steep as the other side we had come up. Nevertheless Scharlie made us stop before the final descent to the bay as she was worried we might not get back up. The view from here was better than anything we were likely to see at the bottom so we parked and sat under a tree.

Stony Bay is a deep inlet, flanked by the bush-clad and sacred hills of Mt Moehau. The water was clear green glass and we could hear an eerie cry from the sea caves; maybe it was seals. To our left was the steep wooded gorge of the valley in Hinawai that we haven't seen and to our right the open ocean

Overlooking the Hinewai Nature Reserve

with crested waves and the white sails of a yacht. We turned round in a scrape or lay-by and drove back slowly past a beach that looked nice, so reversed and went for a paddle on the muddy sand with a flock of oystercatchers. On the way home we bought fish and chips in Christchurch, which were excellent.

Sunday 19 February

On Sunday we had arranged to go to Amberley to visit Raymond Herber's sculpture park, an hour's drive north past Rangiora and Waimakarira River where Steve has to go on Tuesday to interview the Chief Planner for the district. We set off in Kate's husband's old car that Malcolm and Doreen say they use when they come to New Zealand. The weather was poor and it began to rain soon after we arrived while Raymond was giving a demonstration of working with steel on an open forge to a coach load of OAPs, We had been expecting gimcrack, rusty, scrap metal creations but he has great artistic talent. He is working in what was an old cement works and has taken on an immense task but is doing well. He had set up his forge in the large shed previously used for crushing stone and is creating a garden to show his sculptures against the backdrop of the old quarry from which soft

Stony Bay from the col where we picknicked

limestone had been dug for cement and for liming the fields. He lives there with his wife and child and they have planted trees and made a garden as a setting for his work. There was a huge revolving signature work in the centre made from recycled metal that he said someone had offered him a quarter of $1 million for but he refused, saying he needed to keep his key works like this and the huge plough horse that had taken him six months to fashion from mild steel plate which he polished to a gleaming shine and sealed with varnish. He said he used mild steel because stainless steel got work hardened and had to be fashioned in much smaller pieces. He made a poker while he lectured and offered it for $25 which he said was a bargain. It certainly seemed so and one of the youngest of the pensioners put her hand up. Doreen said she had been thinking about buying it for Kate and seemed disappointed. But she mentioned it to Raymond's wife

We wandered around in the drizzle and admired the works. There were a couple of bicycle contraptions you could ride that pedalled through a series of cogs and chains 10 propellers or suchlike. Malcolm jumped on one and we took his picture. Scharlie was very taken by the garden design and by many of the works. In a number he had cunningly used stainless cutlery to represent petals and leaves. We hope he makes a success of it, but he needs some big

Raymond Herber's signature sculpture of a plough horse

commissions. He mentioned that the huge vine leaves propped against a thatched shelter were for the consortium of local vineyards.

On the way back we stopped at Malcolm and Doreen's favourite restaurant and had a salad and managed to get back by three and do some more surveying, this time in the Mount Pleasant area. We are getting more proficient and manage to cover more ground. Andy Buchanan had invited us to have tea at his house so we rang to say we might be a little late. We found it easily, it's quite near Molly and John's – a large old timber house built about 1910 and rather like Leveret Croft in that daylight comes into each room from various sides. But the proportions are more gracious than our home in Derbyshire and they have a large balcony facing west and a marvellous huge gumtree framing the view north. We sat in the lounge and Andy gave us advice about where to walk. He is keen on the Abel Tasman walk and described how you could easily do sections by getting a water taxi to pick you up or drop you off. His wife was keen for us to do the Queen Charlotte walk that she said she liked on the grounds that we were going to Picton to get the ferry, but Andy disagreed. We really liked their house and since they come to England regularly we suggested they get in touch when they were next over. Molly had food ready for us when we got back and we went to bed early.

Malcolm riding bicycle contraption in sculpture park

Monday 20 February

John drove us in again and parked in Ballantyne's, the main department store's, car park. It turned out that the Drexel building, where Steve was due to meet Caroline Inglis, the city planner in charge of the CBD plan, was just round the corner. He had to wait a while but once they got talking he found her to be clear, direct and informative. She rang Bruce Dean, his next appointment

Cutlery sculpture made from knives and forks

at Tonkin and Taylor, and called a taxi. The taxi driver was chatty and Steve

Andy Buchanan's elegant timber house circa 1910

explained what he was doing. When they reached the Bailey building on the other side of the park Steve got out his wallet and realised he hadn't got any money. It was $19. He apologised and said he had given all his money to his wife that morning so she would go shopping in town. He laughed and said the ride was on him. Steve tried to give him US dollars but he refused in the kindest way.

Bruce was good; slightly nerdy but well informed and able to explain what information was being assembled in the GIS and how buildings and zones were being assessed. He went through the story chronologically explaining how he had done his Ph.D. in civil engineering with Andy Buchanan and was setting up his own consultancy in GIS when the September earthquake happened and EQC, the Earthquake Commission, had offered him a job. Tonkin Taylor had insisted he joined their staff rather than freelance.

Steve was supposed to see Rod Cameron from SCIRT, the Stronger Christchurch Infrastructure Rebuild Team, but he rang and had a chat on the phone, then walked through the park in the sunshine to meet Scharlie. She had come in with Molly and John and we found each other in the *Re:Start* arcade. We were most impressed by these colourful shipping container conversions and think they are an asset to the city. Given the numbers of

Anti-capitalism campaign in Hagley Park

Brightly painted shipping container shops in the town centre and girl on piano

Girl paying piano in town centre

people about, many others feel the same. Molly and John had an appointment with their solicitor to redo their wills. John has been working on it all week, prompted by their coming trip to do the Tongariro Crossing trek. So we had a bite in a restaurant in the containers. There was a girl in a dark suit playing classical piano on an electronic piano and a breakdancer doing his thing.

River Avon forms a green winding corridor through city centre

We found the car where John had left it for us and drove to New Brighton and walked on the pier until Steve's five o'clock appointment with Lianne Dalziel, MP for East Christchurch – the part most badly affected by the earthquake with much of it red zoned as unfit for habitation, given the thin crust of stable soil, high water table and risk of flooding. The pier and library, new concrete structures at the seaward end of the shopping avenue that has been pedestrianised, seem very popular – the pier patronised by fishermen, and the library by old folk and schoolchildren. The shops are putting a brave face on events despite what must have been a big drop in trade as many people will have to leave the area and relocate.

Lianne has her consultancy office in a corner shop on the shopping parade and welcomed me into her office. She is energetic and outspoken and seemed pleased to talk. She put a lot of what she regards as slow decision making and lack of effective leadership and co-operation down to politics – both local and national. She reckons that Bob Parker, the mayor, was about to lose the election when the September quake hit and he cancelled campaigning in the name of pulling together for the common good. She also has little time for the Minister, Gerry Brownlee, who she said was a ex woodwork teacher and a bully.

New Brighton pier

Steve rejoined Scharlie who was parked by the water watching the waves while she wrote postcards. We went surveying – our last chance to finish Mount Pleasant – and got a bit lost on the way back, and missed our turn and ended up doing an illegal U-turn on the motorway to Lyttleton just before it entered the tunnel through the mountain. It was a pity, in retrospect, that we hadn't continued since we never did get to see the other side of Port Hills.

Tuesday 21 February

I got up early. It is a long drive to Rangiora and I didn't want to be rushed. John had given me clear instructions that I was able to follow without mishap, navigating the one-way system around the closed city centre and joining the motorway north. Just after crossing the Waimakariri River I turned off and found the council offices quite easily and parked in the street. This is a small quiet place. I was early so I went from a coffee and read the paper. Victoria Caseley, the district council planner, was a serious looking woman in spectacles. She was from the UK and had married a Kiwi and they have a horse farm in the hills near here. She said she was a part-time ambulance driver and had been very occupied with civil defence after the September quake. She

Rangiora High Street

reckoned Waimakariri had been relatively worse affected than Christchurch. I had wondered about the usefulness of driving out all this way but Victoria was very helpful and informative. What I hadn't appreciated was that, despite seemingly having plenty of land to relocate people, much of the flat land between the two rivers is prone to flooding. Developers have already enough land banked to build on but are releasing land for new homes very slowly. There is also an issue about immigrant workers and the temporary housing they need. The government has said it needs to recruit 7000 workers, mainly site managers and skilled craftsmen, and has been advertising principally in the UK. But these people will not be offered permanent residency, which Victoria thinks is a mistake. She said she would have liked to bring over her parents but since she had two siblings in the UK they didn't qualify. If one of her siblings lived in France or if she only had one brother they would have and she didn't think this is right; they wouldn't be a burden on the social services and would cover their own medical and pension costs, she said.

I had an appointment in town and asked for directions back and she said not to worry, she'd like to show me some of the damage and she would come part of the way with me. I could leave her and someone would come and collect her. Going to the car she showed me the parapets on all the buildings

Effects of severe liquefaction

in the high street. Like in the Westerns, it is a fashion here to disguise the gable ended tin-roofed buildings with masonry or concrete parapets, which come detached in large quakes. She showed me the areas near the river in Kaiapoi that had suffered liquefaction and had been red zoned. We drove with me photographing with one hand while steering with the other. She described how people had cleared the mud from their yards three or four times before giving up and leaving. The roads were buckled and the sewage and water mains smashed. They have laid water pipes on the surface and installed Portaloos on every corner. She took me to see two homes that had been cracked open by a fault opening up under the concrete foundation slab. She described how the earthquake had happened in the middle of the night and people had run out their front doors in the pitch black with their house falling down around them and had plunged off their front step up to their necks in slimy mud.

I wondered if this area would ever be habitable again; nice houses some of them had obviously cost a lot. A quiet neighbourhood, a safe place to bring up children, close to the shops in the town centre, close to the country and the river and only half an hour into Christchurch. People would have to start again. Maybe half the residents are still here, still trying to make it work when the smart thing to do is to get all the payment you can and cut and run. That's

Damaged catholic Cathedral, Barbados Street

what the smart investors are doing, she said getting the insurance money for buildings in the centre of Christchurch and investing in the Gold Coast or Auckland.

It was hot when I left Victoria by the side of the road but she was unfazed by the heat and calmly waited for her lift back. I drove back into town and found Jasper Vande Lingen's architects offices easily. They were in an old timber building with elegant high ceilinged rooms, largely unaffected by the quake. He described how he got 20 local firms to cooperate to produce a set of ideas for rebuilding different functions in the centre. They had run a series of public events and exhibitions after the September quake when the council was largely doing little. Then after the February quake they had been shouldered aside, he said. The Minister had thanked them for their document of proposals but has said no thanks and the planners and CERA had taken over. But there is no spatial vision for the reconstruction nor any clear indication of which functions might be relocated, he said, just a set of rules that the developers and owners disagreed with and anyway had a dispensation to ignore for five years. Jasper was a nice gentle man and a good designer and had done well to get architects to collaborate on producing a design vision and the ideas they had developed on their website had largely been copied by the council when

Public consultation by City Council: people wanted a greener, low density city

they had launched the campaign in March following the second quake.

From there I drove up Barbados Street, pass the ruined Catholic Cathedral and got back for a late lunch and a frantic packing before going into town with John and all our luggage to get a hire car and head off for Arthur's Pass.

Arthur's Pass and Bealey Spur

The car was a dream and very relaxing. We opted for full insurance so we didn't need to inspect the car and note any dents and we paid for a full tank of petrol so we could leave it when we arrived at the ferry without needing to fill up. John and Molly had made us feel so at home and it was hard to leave. John guided us out-of-town along Riccarton Road which was very

Saying goodbye to Molly and John who were so generous in hosting our stay

helpful since the one way temporary road systems are very confusing and we set off on the main road north west to the mountains. We passed through the detached suburbs where Dorrie and Tim had been staying and after an hour stopped at the Sheffield pie shop that Malcolm had recommended and bought a steak and mushroom pie and a couple of cakes for supper. The forecast wasn't great but we decided to walk anyway. We had done really well, worked hard all week and now we were off on an adventure, getting away in good time, despite all the things we had to do that day. The plains gave way to mountains and we began to climb. The vegetation changed and we came to a wide alluvial floodplain of the Waimakariri River and passed a sign for Bealey Spur where we thought we might return tomorrow. We crossed the river by a long narrow bridge and entered the gorge of Arthur's Pass and reached the village before dark.

We found the Peet's holiday home, or bach as they are known here, just past the main restaurant. The key worked and we were there. These huts were originally the huts for the miners who were cutting the Otiro Tunnel for the railway line running across the Island from east to west coast to supply the gold rush around Murchison. In the bach there was a large wood stove, two bedrooms kitchen, shower and compost loo. We got the fire lit, unpacked a

The Peet's holiday home or 'bach', Arthur's pass

bit and went in search of food at the restaurant as Scharlie had decided to save the pie till tomorrow. The restaurant had been the home of a German skier who started the tourist industry here. We had fish, which was good. The waitress was chatty and friendly and told us about the history of the place and about the Keas, the big fluffy parrots with the red under wings that destroy car windscreen wipers and door trims. Apparently there is a mob of 20 or so parrots that hang out near the toilet block and bum food off tourists. We walked in the rain up to the waterfall on the way up to Avalanche Peak, then we went to bed in our sleeping bag bags so we wouldn't have to wash the bedding.

Wednesday 22 February

We woke later than we wanted to, but were out of the house soon after 9 checking out the weather at the tourist office, where it forecast heavy rain in the afternoon. We wanted to do Bealey Spur and the Ranger said he had just recommended it to another party. We went for breakfast in the store and finally got rolling after 10 and drove to the turnoff to Bealey. The tarmac section gave access to a couple of dozen baches that dated, like those in

Lighting the fire at Peet's bach

Arthur's Pass, to before the creation of the park. The steep narrow track climbed up through pine woods and it was hard work but we pressed on and passed a couple of elderly Americans who we didn't think would make it and then a British foursome who had just turned back. The wet patches of the track had timber walkways and finally we reached the hut. A young man was lying on one of the bunks. He looked ill and we asked if we could do anything but he said no he'd be okay. We moved to the bench outside and drank some water and rested a little, then set off up the ridge to the summit we could see from the hut. There was a deep wooded gorge to the south and to the north, the Waimakariri River, braided into many channels flowing down a wide level plain. Sitting on a rock and we saw a bright light on the other side of the valley in the east and figured it must be a train on the thin line we could just see on the opposite bank. Finally we picked out the train moving slowly along the pencil line with a red engine at the front. The ridge went on rising gently and we continued to the third summit and were lucky there was still a view before we turned back and it started to spot with the rain.

It seemed a long way down. It always surprises you how much you have managed to climb as you walk down. We asked a French couple to take our photo and ended up with a movie as the settings had changed. The lad had

Steve writing his journal outside hut on Bealey Spur

Descending from the summit in the rain

Lichen draped beech woods on the way back

vacated the hut when we got there and we stopped and had the remainder of our food until a group of three English girls arrived and chased us out. Our feet were hurting by the time we got back to the car but we felt pleased we managed to do something despite the weather. We drove back to the bach and cooked the pie and dried vegetables we had bought in the store and then went lazily to bed.

Abel Tasman trail

Thursday 23 February

In the morning we packed, cleaned and had breakfast early in the store. It was still raining but there were occasional bursts of sunlight. The gorge starts here at Arthurs Pass and it's steep and narrow, which is why the settlement is here where the Otiro tunnel begins. We sailed past a turn off that gave a splendid view with a spectacular waterspout sailing over the road to fall into the river bottom. So we turned round and went back at the first opportunity

Waterfall tumbling over the road in the gorge of Arthur's Pass on our way north

and took photographs in the rain. There were slow log lorries with trailers that were most courteous pulling in when they could to let traffic pass. There were also a few motorbikes, mainly Harley-Davidson tourers. We left the road

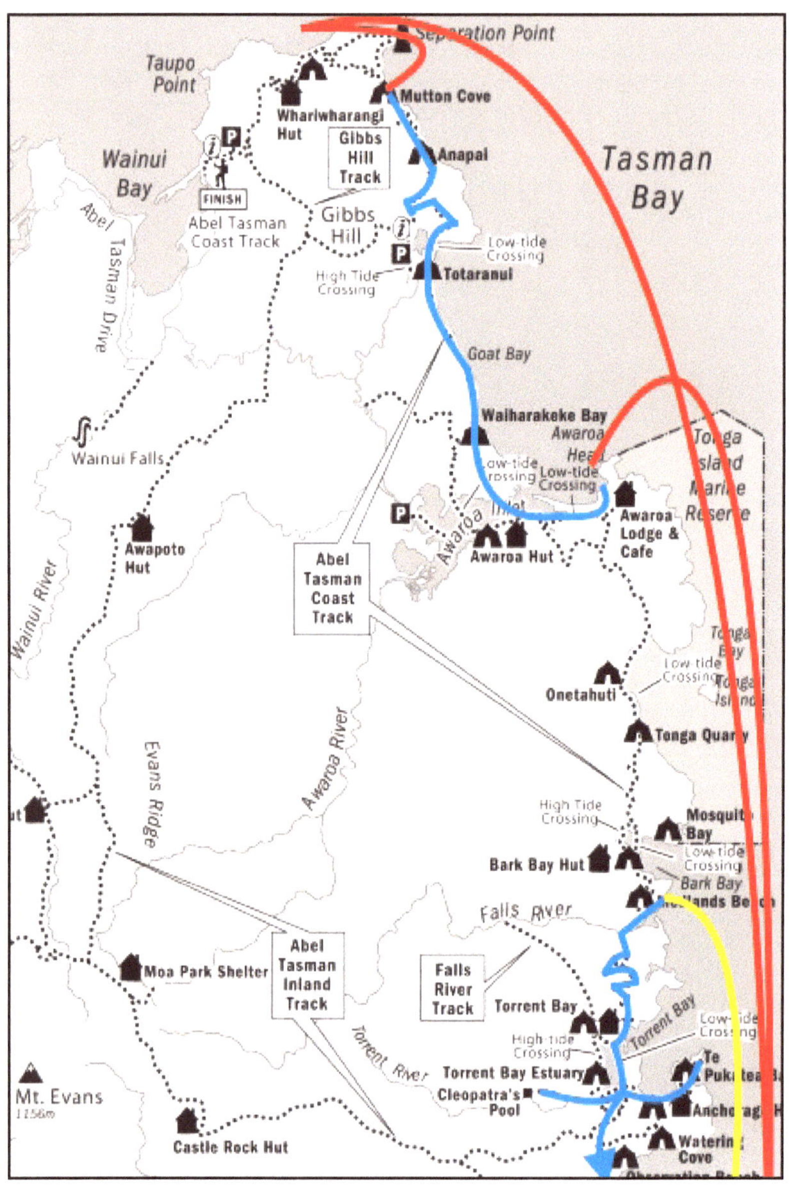

Abel Tasman trail: red water taxi; yellow kayak; blue walk

to Greymouth and turned north towards Murchison and the gold fields. The railway goes this way and we kept pace with a train for a while. This is lush cattle ranch country and we stopped in Murchison for lunch at a cafe. We have been most impressed by the food here – it's so much fresher and tastier than we had expected.

We spotted a little local history museum while we had been driving round and thought we had time to visit. It was rather delightful and full of bric-a-brac – old telephones, dentistry equipment, crockery, household implements, crystals, rock samples, photographs and paintings. We were interested in the accounts of early life in the town and in the records of historic earthquakes in New Zealand in 1848, 1855 and 1888. A man late in life had narrated his life as a boy in the town – how isolated they had been and how the carters had brought provisions from Nelson on steep mountain tracks, often drunk if they were transporting beer or spirits. He described their ingenuity in tapping kegs and bottles and disguising the thefts. He'd run the general store and related how he dealt with the hundred or so Chinese miners panning for gold, how honest they were and how none had cheated him. He said little about the European miners. The account of the earthquake was also fascinating. The narrator, a young man, had helped with the rescue and gone to Nelson with

Murchison local history mueum

his father to give news and get help. Again one is struck by how isolated these places were, how vulnerable to natural disasters and how resilient the folk were. We pressed on, passing through hop and vine country, then fruit – apples, pears, plums, and after a long stretch through the mountains and forests of the Kahurangi National Park, following the course of the muddy Buller River until finally reaching Motueka on Tasman Bay.

Scharlie wanted to stop at a tourist agency but we pressed on to Marahau and found a water taxi firm on the main corner and got a brochure. We were worried about petrol – the gauge has suddenly dropped to nearly zero but we were told we could buy petrol at Aqua Taxis on the road. We drove on looking for somewhere to stay and Scharlie spotted a sign for Abel Tasman Stables B&B with a nice garden drive up to a house with a view. George, the proprietor, said he had an exchange student in the room he thought would do for us. The deal was that the student would move out if visitors came. He said to give him time to clear it while we went for petrol.

Where we bought petrol, we booked a water taxi to Anchor Bay the next day with a walk back to Marahau, this being the first stage of the Abel Tasman walk. George made tea and crackers with tomato. We unpacked and walked to the Park restaurant George recommended. It was rustic, with a large

Bridge over River Marahau

shaded patio and indoor area with stage and bar. Tonight is open mike night and we thought we'd stay and see if it was any good. We found a lovely table overlooking the garden with a view through the bar to the ocean. The meal was fabulous. We ordered seafood fettuccine and the mussels, clams, scallops and winkles were the freshest we'd ever tasted – as if they had just been pulled from the sea. No wonder we've had trouble with seafood in the past; it wasn't fresh. The light went, it got chilly and we moved inside and found a nice seat in a corner and Scharlie ordered a pudding. The first act, a young man with long curly black hair and an extravagant moustache and black waistcoat was good, but the following acts were out of key so we gave up and walked home arm in arm in the dark guided by a million unfamiliar stars. Only Orion we recognised, and he was upside down.

George asked us what we had booked for the day and then convinced us that we should be more ambitious and take the taxi to the far end of the park and do the last stretch of the walk from Mutton Cove to Awaroa Head – he rang the taxi firm and arranged for us to change.

Park Restaurant Marahau

Friday 24 February

We had booked to leave at 9am and had to be there by 8.30. We arrived in good time and waited for our boat to arrive on its trailer pulled by a tractor. Scharlie posed for a photo and the camera battery gave out. We had only 10 minutes and Scharlie was worried that there was no time to go back for a spare battery because we had left the car at the B&B and walked. Steve thought he had just enough time if he ran and made it halfway back before he had to walk and catch his breath. He found a spare battery and the car keys and drove back and parked with a minute to spare.

The tractor drove the boat into the water and it floats! The tidal range is 4 metres and at low water the tide is half a mile out. It was high water and we were soon off. Our driver, Andy, was a chunky, ruddy-faced Kiwi with a sense of humour and a lively line of patter. At one point he admonished our fellow passengers for not listening closely to his commentary. Scharlie had been worried she might be seasick, but the boat bounced rather than rolled and she was fine. The first stretch to Torrent Bay was quite calm, but when we left Onetahuti Bay on the last lap to Totaranui it was quite rough and Andy put us on another boat saying he didn't want to subject the other passengers to the rough conditions unnecessarily. We wondered if we'd make it, but the next

Water taxi

stretch to Mutton Cove wasn't as bad and our new driver was more laid-back. He drove us around the rocks of Mutton Cove to see the seal pups and had a much better view than with Andy on Tonga Island, which is supposed to be the best place to see seals. He also went round Separation Point into Golden Bay just to show us what it was like.

A lad who had been going to disembark with us discovered he left his water bottle at the last beach and decided to stay on board. The two of us waded ashore like the Dutch navigator Abel Tasman in December 1642, bashed the sand from our sandals and set off up the narrow track from the beach. The walk wound its way along the coast through tall tree ferns, forest and shorter scrub, sometimes following the headline and sometimes dropping to a sandy cove or white sand beach. It was delightful and being so far from Marahau, we practically had the track to ourselves and were in a kind of paradise. The weather was perfect, a light breeze, balmy temperature and divine views; we couldn't believe our luck. We found a beach for lunch and spread ourselves along the sun bleached logs. We ate cheese and biscuits, stripped off to our underwear – we had lost our swimming costumes in Perth – and stretched out lengthways along the log and sunbathed. We had to be back in time to catch

Seals basking in sunshine at Mutton Cove

The common cormorant or shag (lays eggs inside a paper bag)

Lunch spot on Anapai beach

Mutton Cove to Totaranui

Scharlie about to wade across Awaroa Creek and soak her camera

the water taxi at 3.15 and were running out of time as we approached the last bay, so instead of taking the longer inland track we took a chance on the quicker way across the river estuary, the Awaroa Inlet, by the most direct line. The tide had gone out a long way but the river still looked deep. Scharlie was keen so she waded in wearing her shorts, while Steve stripped off and put his clothes in his pack which he carried on his head. The water came above his waist at one point and he stumbled and nearly fell. He reached the opposite bank and pulled on his clothes as Scharlie discovered she had got the camera, which had been in a case around her neck, was wet through. Despite drying the battery and chip in the sun we couldn't make it work.

We ate the last of the fruit while waiting for the water taxi and when we got back to Marahau, the boat drove straight onto the trailer and the tractor started up with hardly a break in momentum. That evening we'd arranged to eat at the B&B with George and the three help exchange lads, two from France and Stevie, a confident personable lad from China who was apple picking to pay his way and planned a career in marketing. We got to know each other over chicken and roast potatoes and peas.

Water taxi drives straight onto trailer and is towed in by tractor

Saturday 25 February

The following morning we were booked on a canoe trip from Marahau to Whispering Cove, just before the Anchorage Peninsula. We found our guide, a bouncy blonde Kiwi called Dawn, who showed us the ropes of how to put on the lifejacket and cockpit cover, how to stow the gear in the waterproof compartments and funniest of all, how to paddle by standing behind each other in pairs and paddling in the car park. We loaded the kayaks on a trailer and headed off for the beach. Steve had his camera in a waterproof map case round his neck and was able to take some pictures once we got going. It wasn't difficult paddling and we were able to make good progress and keep up with the other four boats. We headed across the wide Bay, following the buoys that indicated slightly deeper water and once clear of the bay, cut to the coast and followed it north. Dawn had to meet some other people at 12 and maybe we had started a little late because she drove us on and we got there early.

We planned to walk over the headland into Anchorage Bay and explore the peninsula that George had recommended. It was quite a way down and there was a luxury house on a prominent site overlooking the bay and we wondered how they got permission to build there. Scharlie changed her mind and wanted to walk west to Cleopatra's Pool inside of the peninsula, so we set

Kayaking from Marahao to Whispering Cove

off back up the hill after walking along the beach to the DOC hut and loos. It was hot and not as nice as the previous day's walk and Steve's feet had begun to rub badly in the sandals. The trail seemed to go on and on, so Scharlie asked a young lad how much further and he said another 20 minutes, so we turned back and retraced our steps. The walk was a bit of a pain – there were many more people walking this stretch, there were fewer views and nowhere

Torrent Bay

to sit and rest. We finally found a turn off down to a promontory and found a place to have lunch. As we approached Marahau there was a way down to Tinline Bay and made our way across the exposed mudflats to the entrance to the park and a short walk back to the B&B. George kindly let us use his own shower – there were new guests in our room – and all our gear was piled up in his living room. We quickly sorted ourselves out, paid, packed and set off to Richmond to stay with Bridget, John Andreae's sister.

It was a short drive just over an hour and the last stretch over a flooded estuary looked interesting and we went back here the following morning to Rabbit Island beach. We found Oxford Street and Bridget's place easily. It's a nice house, modern and well designed, and Bridget moved here from Auckland when her daughter remarried, to be near her best friend. She is small and of similar birdlike physique as her brother but she is much more chatty and she and Scharlie started talking about family, life in India, Mussoorie, where she lived as a girl, about her stepmother, Lois, Scharlie's aunt, and about her own children and grandchildren. Molly had told us that Bridget hated cooking and entertaining but she had prepared cold meat and boiled potato salad and coleslaw which was fine. They don't use duvets but interleave a blanket between two white, ironed sheets. It was the same at Molly's, all beautifully tucked in. What careful work!

Elephant rock

Wellington

Sunday 26 February

We asked if she'd like us to strip the bed. No leave it just as it is, then I can decide when I feel like doing it, she said. We got a good night's sleep and were dawdling. Bridget wanted some advice about pruning a large magnolia grandiflora in her back garden. I understand the principle but I'm just not sure the amount, she said. Scharlie thought she should be bold and take the whole thing down. Steve left her in the hot sun with a pair of secateurs and a large hat. We had aimed to leave by 1:30 pm but Bridget said wistfully, I wish you could come to Rabbit Island, you could find more shells when we walk along the beach. How far is it? Only 15 minutes. Steve was nervous, but Bridget was enthusiastic. She served bread and cheese and salad with alacrity and we were in the car in double quick time, Bridget giving chirpy directions from the back. Through the suburbs, pleasant houses set in English looking gardens – some housing beginning to creep up the mountain sides, following the highway back the way we came, right to Rabbit Island, picnic areas under hot sun and trees, eucalyptus groves and avenues down to a long beach. We walked along the

Marahao

sand sharing her delight. There were lots of shells and Steve found the best one yet. I'm glad you've seen more of Havelock than just my house, Bridget said, and we felt glad too. It's time to go; we drop Bridget off, she's going to the cinema with her friend Sue, a quick visit to the loo and check around and we find Steve's shoes behind the door.

We leave just after 1.30 and are supposed to check-in by 4.30 in Picton; we had allowed 4 hours for the drive so felt stressed. The drive goes through Nelson and then winds up through the mountains before reaching flatter wine country south of Picton. The traffic is slow through Hamilton, then onto the motorway for a brief spurt before the highway swings onto mounting loops as it climbs inland through the coastal range. Through places like Wakapuaka and Whagamoa – places to pause and walk and swim and listen to birds, but no time. When we reached the plains the road straightened and we moved down a fertile valley – pastures with cows grazing, the mountains standing like a guard of honour on either side; apple and pear orchards, kiwifruit and vines. The road was fast and we got to Picton in good time. The hire car guy was most relaxed, telling us to park in the terminal car park and drop the keys in a hole on the desk in the terminal building. We checked in the bags – such an improvement on ferries we've taken in Europe where we've had to lug heavy

Bridget and Scharlie on Rabbit Island beach Nelson

luggage up and down six flights of steep metal stairs. We had time to kill so we parked in the shopping street in town and had a look in the shops and walked along the front. Scharlie bought a carry on bag to take all her stuff and we looked at jewellery – particularly something called ruby rock.

We found seats near the prow where we could get a good view and went out on deck and waited. A small prop plane entered the fiord and headed for the port. It landed on floats and taxied straight up onto a trailer like the Aqua taxis and was towed up and away. That's the way to travel, we thought, maybe he commutes to work this way. The passage was delightfully smooth. Initially you sail along the Queen Charlotte Sound, weaving a path through its many islands and finally reaching the open sea through a gap between two rocky headlands not much wider than the boat. Across the water clearly visible we could see the mountains of North Island. Scharlie had been dreading Cook Strait as Bridget had said it was very windy at Rabbit Island and that we could have flown from Nelson airport, only 10 minutes away. But the boat hardly rolled in the swell, seeming to glide as if on glass, and we reached Wellington as it drew dark and followed the harbour lights into Island Bay. It was a scramble for taxis, which was rather a surprise after the efficiency to date. But finally we got one and got to the hotel on Cuba Street and went to bed.

Leaving Queen Charlotte Sound and entering Cook Strait separating North and South Island

Monday 27 February

We found a great cafe a couple of hundred yards down Cuba Street to have breakfast – a huge bowl of muesli and fresh fruit with coffee. Scharlie went to the museum while Steve caught a bus out to the GNS Science offices to the north-east of the city to meet Andrew King, the New Zealand earthquake guru. Although his field is not about post earthquake recovery, he was most helpful and informative and filled in some of the background to the decision making in New Zealand. We had lunch in the cafeteria and Andrew ran me back into town to meet Andrew Charlton in the Department of Architecture. Andrew teaches structures and earthquake proof housing to architects. He was friendly and impressed by our walks. When he learnt of Scharlie's interest in gardening he said we must go and see the Wilton Reserve before we left. He said there would be time that evening.

Scharlie arrived back at the hotel 10 minutes after me full of what she had seen in Museum, saying we should go back tomorrow before the flight. She had found her way easily down Cuba Street and along the front to a large new building on the waterfront dedicated to education, conservation and fostering good relations between the Maori and other New Zealanders. She learned a lot about Maori history and her understanding of the landscape began to fall

Sea plane landing in Picton harbour

into place. Steve told her about the reserve, the Wilton Wilderness Park. We caught a bus; it was a sunny evening and we took one of the walks around the reserve, one of the few remnants of Bush to have been rescued. It's a beautiful tranquil place in the midst of suburbia, heavily wooded slopes above the stream, the only unfortunate thing being that power lines cross the reserve, spoiling the view with pylons. The park was founded by a settler who loved the bush and set aside some of his land to preserve the native flora and fauna. He and his wife are buried under a large rock in the park. Now the reserve is under the care and protection of the city council and recently, under the guidance of a botanist, they have begun to document and preserve wild plant species.

On our way up to the hotel we spotted a Malay restaurant that looked good and booked a table. It was good, and cheap and very popular and later we walked up to Florentines, a more expensive and elegant restaurant and had coconut pancetta pudding and wine.

Tuesday 28 February

Our flight to Sydney didn't leave until the early afternoon, so we decided to squeeze in a visit to the museum together. Steve woke with an intense crick in his neck and was in pain as we set off. The museum was marvellous, the

Breakfast in Cuba Street

exhibits were superb and the curation and explanation excellent. We learned how the Maori had colonised New Zealand from Polynesia 600 years before Europeans. There was one of their war canoes and three longhouses or Marae they have reassembled here with the blessing of the Maori people. Scharlie was particularly taken by a life mask of the chief. It is the chiefs who have facial tattoos that describe both their tribal history and their personal character. Another room houses the Waitangi Treaty and recorded interviews with people. Maori activists have recently joined conservationists to invoke the treaty and dispute the way coastal resources have been exploited as fishing and the mining of sand dunes, has, for example, resulted in the destruction of plants used for weaving.

Steve said we had to blow £60 in New Zealand dollars and Scharlie thought how nice to buy the green stone pendant she had picked out yesterday. Greenstone is central to Maori culture. But she baulked at the price, which was more than we had left, so she didn't buy it. Later she regretted it, as the pendant would have been a lovely reminder of the holiday. Back at the hotel we finished packing and hauled the bags down to bus stop and it was spotting with rain as we left for the airport and our flight to Sydney. It was sad saying goodbye to New Zealand.

Remnant of bush in Wilton Wilderness Park

Museum of New Zealand Te Papa Tongarewa. Cable Street Wellington

www.ingramcontent.com/pod-product-compliance
Lightning Source LLC
LaVergne TN
LVHW052258100826
845147LV00001B/84

* 9 7 8 0 9 9 5 7 6 8 0 6 2 *